MW00904387

Vivid Visions

INSPIRATIONAL QUOTES COLORING BOOK FOR ADULTS

By Kim Busbea

This Coloring Book
Belongs to

TEST YOUR COLORS HERE

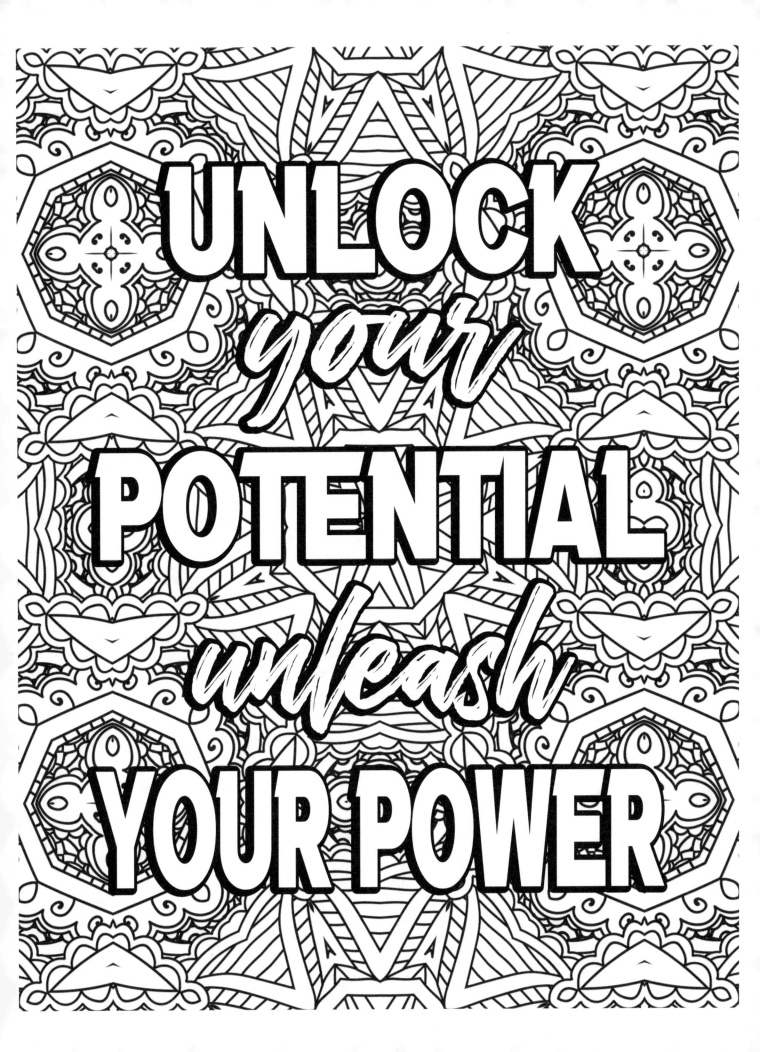

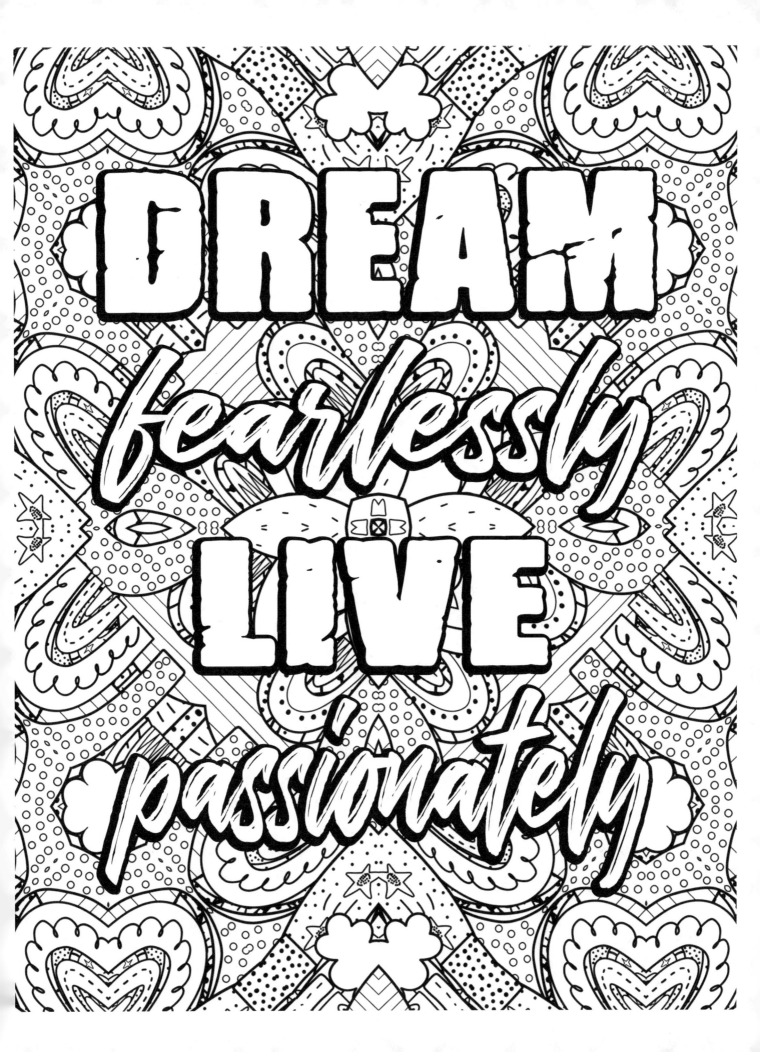

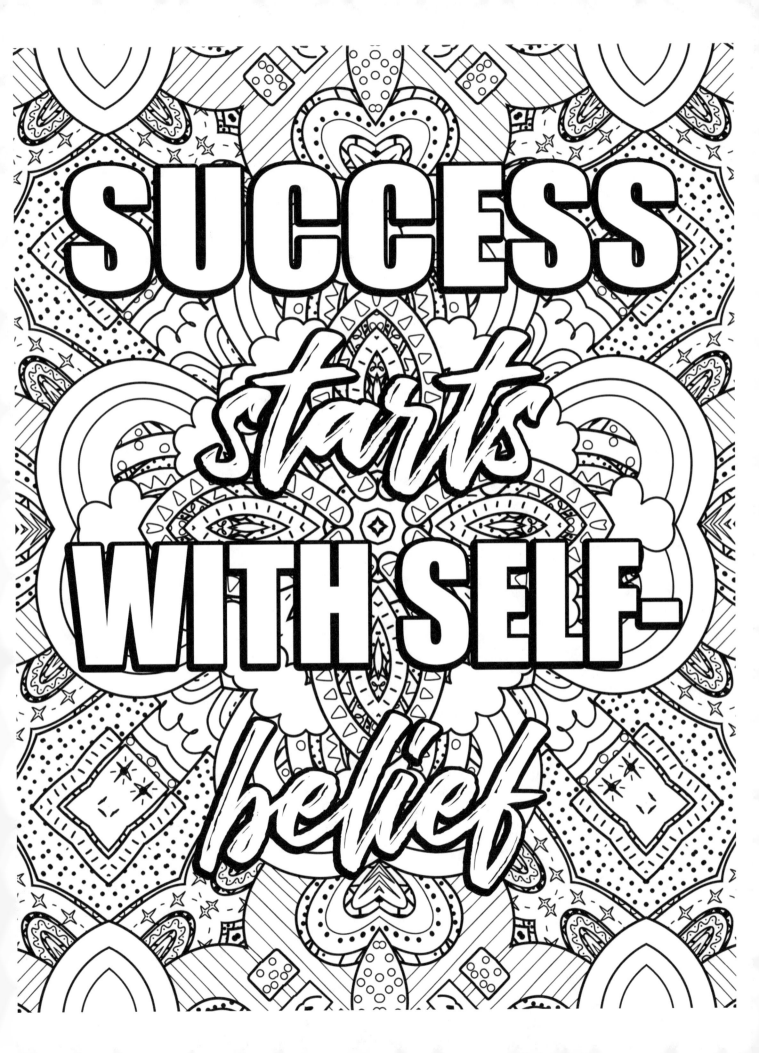

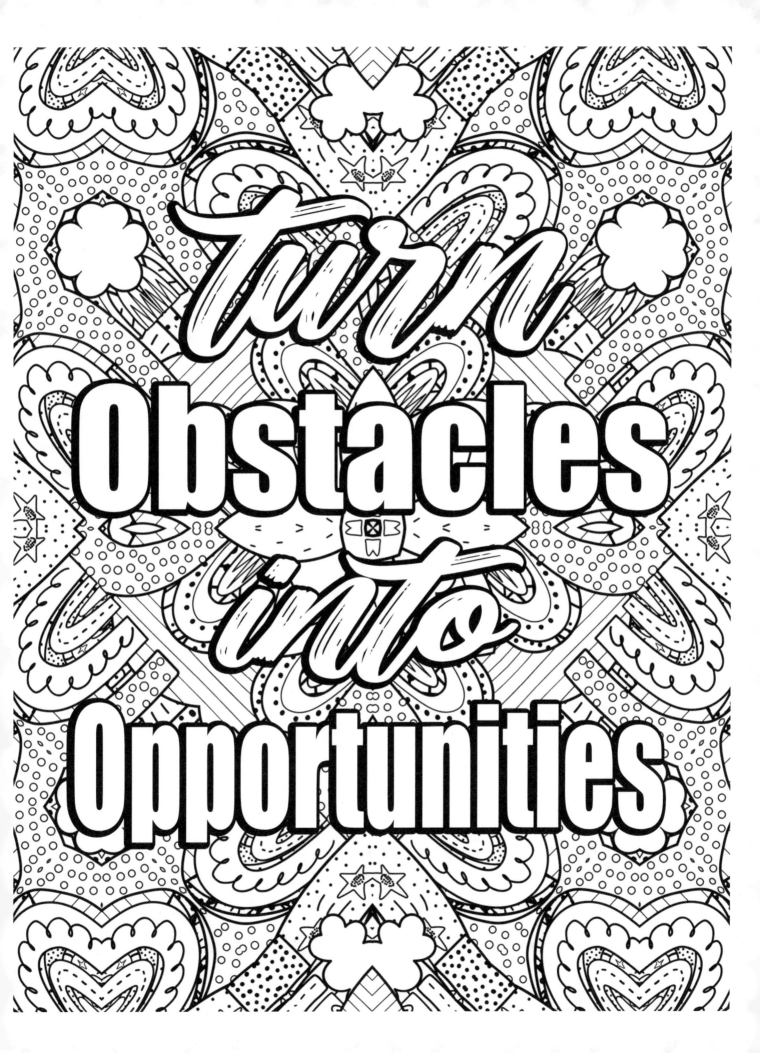

BELIEVE

achieve

SUCCEED

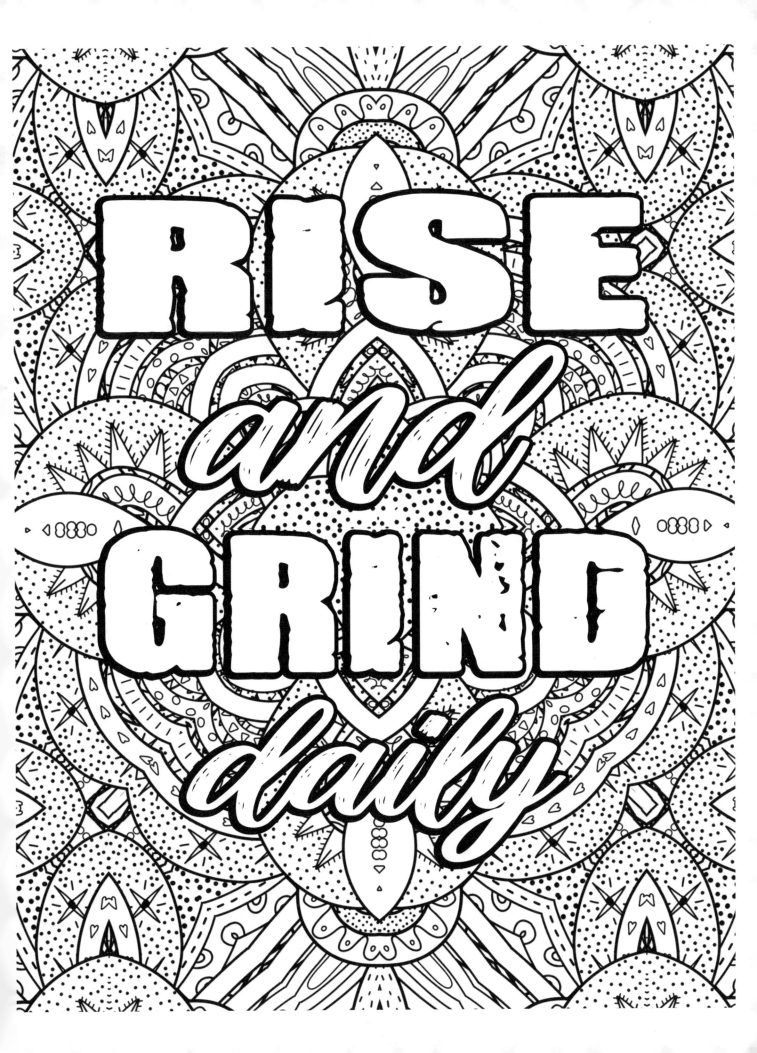

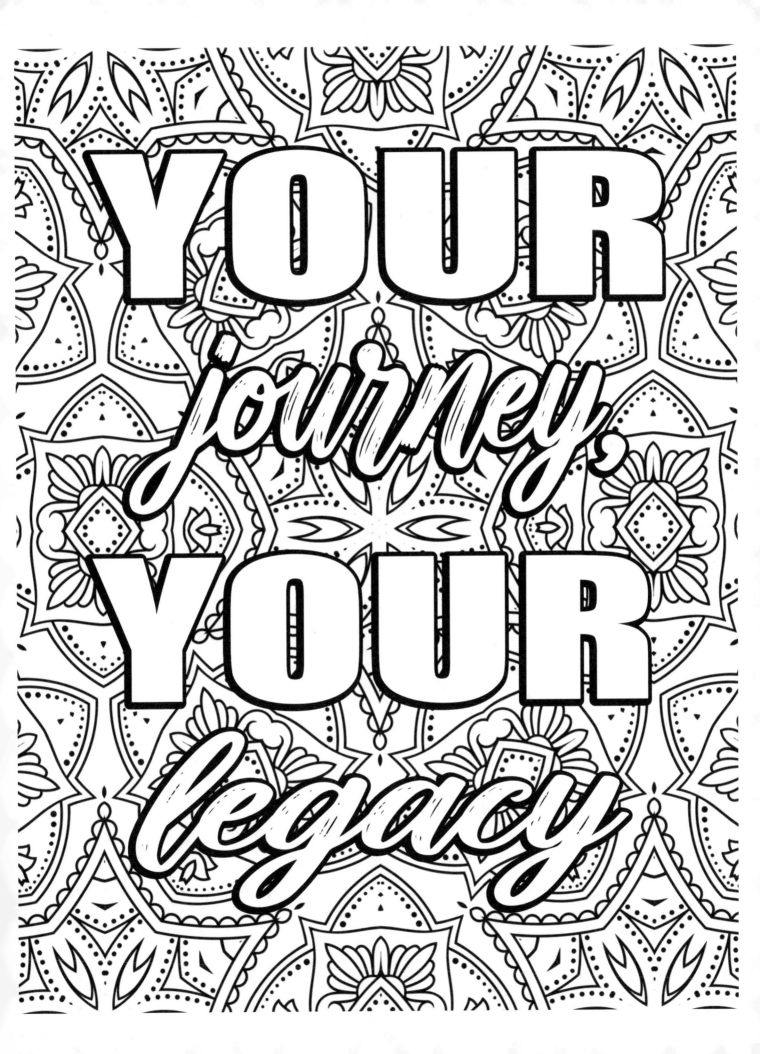

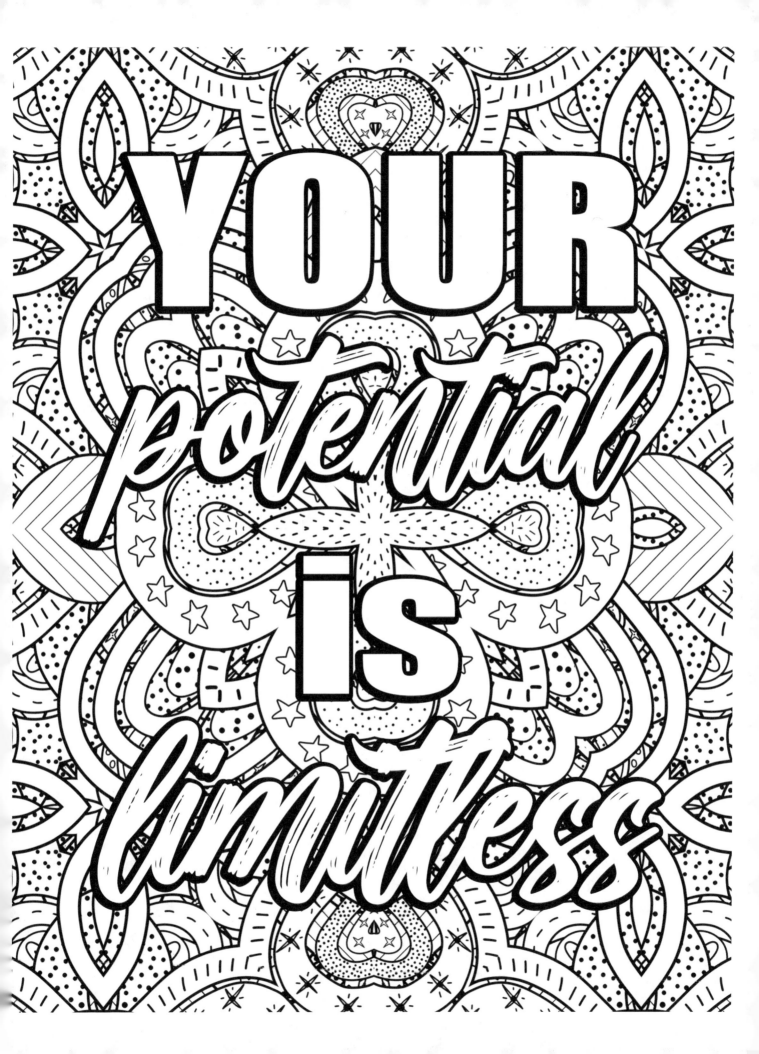

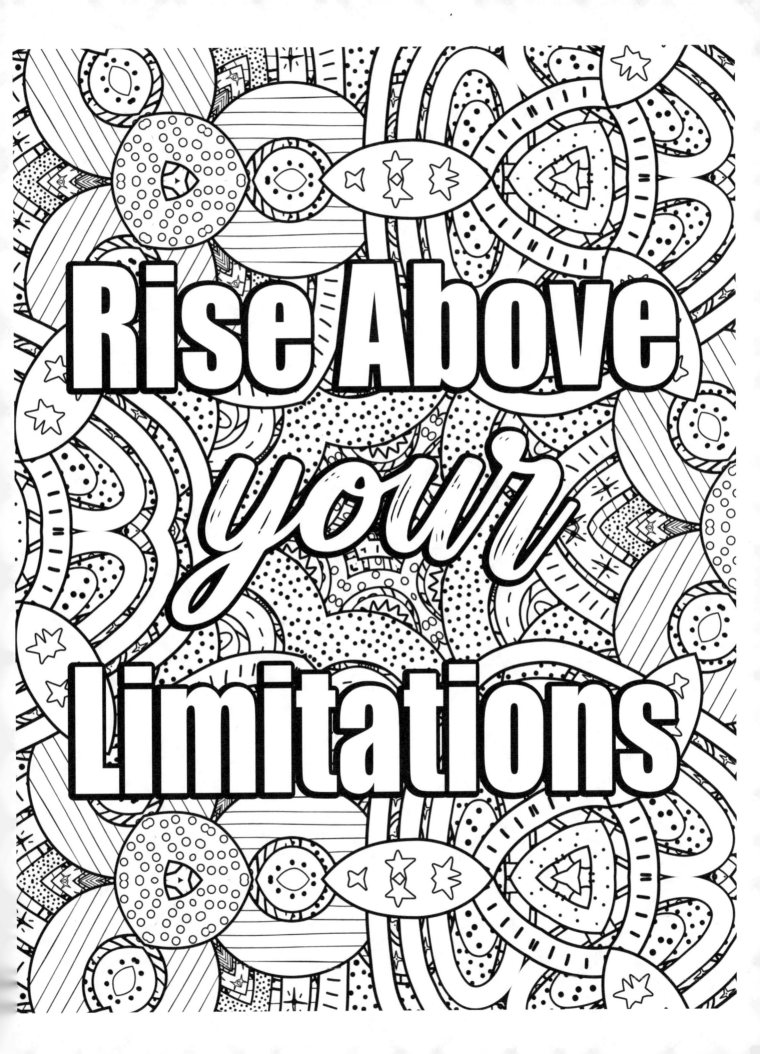

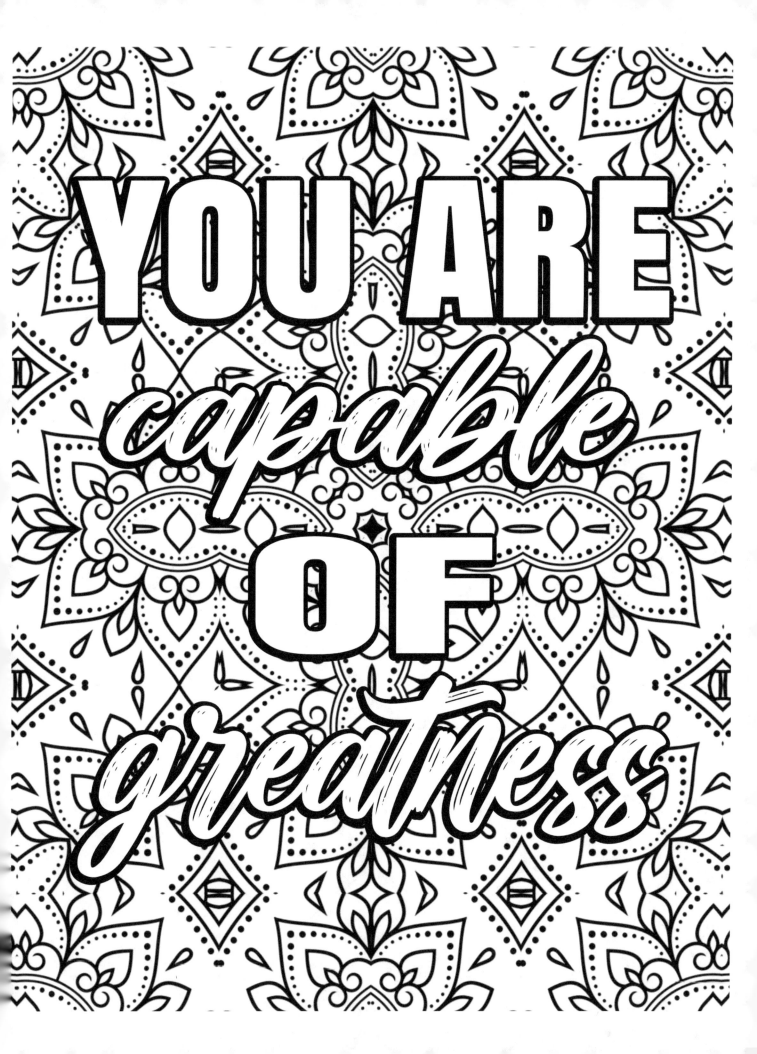

Thank You

FOR YOUR

Please Share Your Feedback

Thank you for purchasing our "Vivid Visions: Inspirational Quotes in Color" If you enjoyed the coloring book, we would be grateful if you could take a few minutes to leave a review on the platform you purchased it from. Your feedback and thoughts about the book would be appreciated and will help us continually improve and reach more people who love coloring. Thanks again for your support.

Made in the USA
Columbia, SC
29 December 2024

48468771R00059